· LEARN ·
JAPANESE
for Beginners

M000086535

LEARN
Katakana

STUDY GUIDE & WRITING PRACTICE

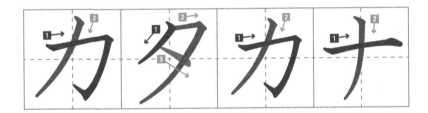

© Copyright 2020 George Tanaka
All Rights Reserved

POLYSCHOLAR

www.polyscholar.com

CONTENTS

Tip: *This book works best with gel pens, pencils, biros and similar media. Take care with markers and ink, as heavy or wet media may result in paper bleed or transfer through to the pages below. Here are some test boxes to check how suitable your pens will be:*

FURTHER JAPANESE

Learning to read, write and speak Japanese is much more simple might at first seem. **Katakana** is the second script we learn and it shares lots of rules wth the first, *Hiragana*. This book has been designed to make it **easier** and **quicker** to get to grips with.

We will start with a brief overview of the Japanese language system, in case you haven't already completed our **Learn Hiragana Workbook**. After a brief look at the different 'alphabets' *(yes, there is more than one!)* we'll jump straight into learning Katakana!

HOW TO USE THIS BOOK

As with learning any language, repetition is one of the fastest ways to soak it up. The second part of this workbook contains lots of carefully-designed instruction pages to help you learn how to write each character, with space to practice your Japanese writing skills:

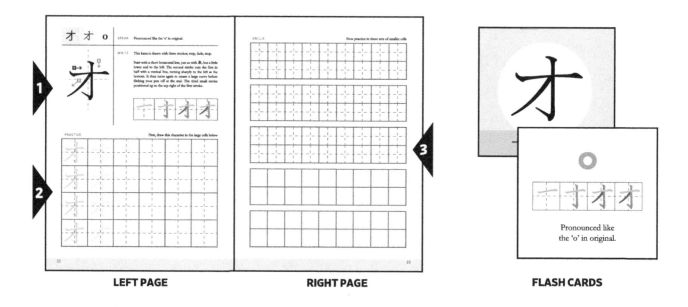

| LEFT PAGE | RIGHT PAGE | FLASH CARDS |

The third part of this workbook contains additional grids that you can use after you have learned how to write some *(or even all)* of the Katakana. These pages are often referred to traditionally as *Genkouyoushi (or* 原稿用紙 *in Japanese)* which means 'manuscript paper'.

The final part of this workbook contains a set of flash card style pages that can either be photocopied or cut out. They are a great way to help you memorize the symbols and test your knowledge. Younger learners should seek help from an adult to cut them out!

JAPANESE SCRIPTS

As you learn Japanese, you will encounter four very different types of scripts *(or alphabets)*. While this might sound complicated, this will start to make more sense in a moment - especially as you will already understand one of them!

RŌMAJI ロマンジ

Literally meaning 'roman letters', this is really just a representation of the Japanese language using familiar English letters. It is only used to translate the language into a form that non-Japanese speakers can understand. It is not that common in every day use.

The other three scripts, **Hiragana**, **Katakana**, and **Kanji**, are used all the time and they are typically combined to make words and sentences in everyday Japanese writing. Each script has it's own purpose and together they tell us what word mean, where they come from, and also how we should say it.

HIRAGANA ひらがな

あいうえおかきくけこ

This is the first script we should learn and it consists of simple characters made with *round* shapes. Unlike the English alphabet, it is a **phonetic script** and each character represents a syllable sound. Each time you see a specific character, you will know how it sounds.

KATAKANA カタカナ

アイウエオカキクケコ

This is also a simple phonetic script. Katakana **represent the same syllable sounds as Hiragana** but are used for words *loaned* from other languages, such as foreign names, modern technology, or foods for example. Their appearance is more *angular and spikey.*

KANJI 漢字

Translated as 'Chinese letters', **Kanji** are characters borrowed from the Chinese language. Unlike the other scripts that represent sounds, **Kanji** symbols show blocks of meaning, like whole words, or a general idea about something.

年 本 月 生 米 前 合 事 社 京

There are literally *thousands* of Kanji, and new ones are being created all the time, so they are quite a challenge for even the most advanced linguists. There is some logic to how they are made so *eventually* you can understand or guess symbols you haven't seen before.

A LOOK AT KATAKANA

Just as with Hiragana, there are **46 basic Katakana** characters that, unlike English letters, represent different spoken sounds. These sounds are the same as Hiragana and are based on just 5 'vowels sounds'. They also have the same consonant-sound counterparts.

Katakana	ア	イ	ウ	エ	オ
Romaji	a	i	u	e	o
Pronunciation	'ah'	'ee'	'oo'	'eh'	'oh'

The Five Vowel Sounds

This book will show you how to write all the basic Katakana and also how extra sounds can be created by combining the basic symbols. By the end of the book, you will be able to write the characters that make up most of the sounds you will need for Japanese.

The next few pages contain a lot of information but try not to let this overwhelm you. In addition to the chart of basic Katakana that you will learn, we will break down some of the basic rules to combining these symbols. And then, we'll put pen to paper!

Katakana Chart

This chart shows the 46 basic Katakana with a *spelling* in Romaji for a similar phonetic sound. The vowel sounds are at the top and their counterpart versions with consonant sounds are shown below them. **note the exception 'n' - also, *wo is an uncommon kana.*

Vowel Sounds

Consonants	a	i	u	e	o
	ア a	イ i	ウ u	エ e	オ o
k	カ ka	キ ki	ク ku	ケ ke	コ ko
s	サ sa	シ shi	ス su	セ se	ソ so
t	タ ta	チ chi	ツ tsu	テ te	ト to
n	ナ na	ニ ni	ヌ nu	ネ ne	ノ no
h	ハ ha	ヒ hi	フ fu	ヘ he	ホ ho
m	マ ma	ミ mi	ム mu	メ me	モ mo
y	ヤ ya		ユ yu		ヨ yo
r	ラ ra	リ ri	ル ru	レ re	ロ ro
w	ワ wa		ン **n		ヲ *wo

DIACRITICS

In addition to the *basic Katakana*, here are 25 **Diacritic** symbols. These are used for similar sounding syllables that are voiced differently. They are essentially the same basic symbols but with extra marks to show they should be pronounced with a slightly altered sound:

Basic	*with Dakuten*	*with Handakuten*

Basic Katakana with these small strokes *(Dakuten)* or a circle *(Handakuten)* above them show that the consonant part of the sound needs to be changed when spoken:

- **k**-sound are pronounced with a **g**-sound.
- **s**-sounds change to a **z**-sound *(except for し)*.
- **t**-sounds become **d**-sounds.
- **h**-sounds become **b**-sounds with *Dakuten*.
  ...or **P**-sounds with the *Handakuten*.

	a	i	u	e	o
k ▶ g	ガ ga	ギ gi	グ gu	ゲ ge	ゴ go
s ▶ z	ザ za	ジ ji	ズ zu	ゼ ze	ゾ zo
t ▶ d	ダ da	ヂ dzi (ji)	ヅ dzu	デ de	ド do
h ▶ b	バ ba	ビ bi	ブ bu	ベ be	ボ bo
h ▶ p	パ pa	ピ pi	プ pu	ペ pe	ポ po

DIGRAPHS

This set of symbols are called **Digraphs** - By using two basic characters we have already seen, they show where two syllable sounds are combined to create a new one:

キ + ヤ = キャ
(ki)   (ya)   (kya)

When writing these letters, it is vital that the second symbol is drawn noticeably smaller than the first. This is how we can tell that the two sounds should be combined.

Pronunciation of these so-called *compound Katakana* sounds is quite simple - for example, キ (ki) + ヤ (ya) becomes キャ (kya) and we pronounce it like 'kiya' *without the 'i' sound.*

Don't let the chart below scare you - all of the Digraphs are made *exclusively* with letters from the イ/i column *(excluding itself)* **and** they are only modified by letters from row **Y**!

キャ *kya*	キュ *kyu*	キョ *kyo*		ギャ *gya*	ギュ *gyu*	ギョ *gyo*
シャ *sha*	シュ *shu*	ショ *sho*		ジャ *ja*	ジュ *ju*	ジョ *jo*
チャ *cha*	チュ *chu*	チョ *cho*		ニャ *nya*	ニュ *nyu*	ニョ *nyo*
ニャ *hya*	ヒュ *hyu*	ヒョ *hyo*		ビャ *bya*	ビュ *byu*	ビョ *byo*
ピャ *pya*	ピュ *pyu*	ピョ *pyo*		リャ *rya*	リュ *ryu*	リョ *ryo*
ミャ *mya*	ミュ *myu*	ミョ *myo*				

DOUBLE CONSONANTS

Some Japanese words contain a *double consonant sound*. Just as with Hiragana, when written in Katakana these words contain an extra symbol in the form of a small ツ / **tsu** *(called sokuon)* to show that it needs to be pronounced differently. Let's look at an example:

ペット

(pe t← to)

petto

Without the small ツ *(tsu)*, the word ペト *(peto)* doesn't have any meaning but ペット *(petto)*, with the *sokuon*, means **pet** - like a hamster or cat!

Notice that the small ツ is placed **before** the character that it takes the extra consonant sound from. When you see words with this modifier, the consonant part of the symbol that follows it *(in this example, the 't' from 'to')* is added to the end of the sound before it.

Both consonants need to be heard separately when the word is spoken, like saying **'pet-to'** but without leaving a gap than can be heard.

LONG VOWEL SOUNDS

We need to be aware of elongated vowel sounds too *(e.g. aa, ii. oo, ee, and uu)*. When spoken, we simply extend the duration of the sound (usually double) but when written in Katakana we use a line ー *(called 伸ばし棒 which literally means 'stretching bar')*.

This is one way Katakana differs from Hiragana, aside from the shapes, as that uses an additional vowel symbol to denote a long vowel sound. Let's look at some examples:

フ + リ = フリー
(fu) (ri)—   **fu-rii** *(free)*

ケ + キ = ケーキ
(ke)— (ki)   **kee-ki** *(cake)*

It is worth noting that the 'stretching bar' is rotated to a vertical line when text is written vertically.

WRITING DIRECTION

Traditionally, Japanese text was arranged in vertical columns and written/read one column at a time from top to bottom and starting at the right side of the page. Since the end of the Second World War, the more familiar horizontal orientation is used - read left to right, just as in the English language. This applies to each of the different scripts.

The text in these examples is identical, except for the reading and writing direction:

私は犬を飼っています。
彼女は行儀が良い。
彼らは寝るのが好きです。
多くの場合、一日中。
多分彼女は怠け者です。

Tategaki
縦書き
(*'vertical writing'*)

私は犬を飼っています。
彼女は行儀が良い。
彼らは寝るのが好きです。
多くの場合、一日中。
多分彼女は怠け者です。

Yokogaki
横書き
(*'horizontal writing'*)

Both of these styles are accepted and are often chosen based on the layout and design of the document. Generally speaking, vertical layouts are used for traditional texts, while horizontal text is found in more modern, official documents or writing. One thing to remember is that books with the *tategaki* vertical writing style are bound the opposite way to English books, so you actually start reading them from the back cover to the front!

PRONUNCIATION

Learning to pronounce Japanese well begins with *Hiragana* and continues with **Katakana** too, as both scripts represent the same sounds when spoken. It's important to practice at this early stage if you want to develop a natural and native sounding accent.

Note: This workbook includes a very basic introduction to Japanese pronunciation, as this is taught most effectively with audio. Each of the practice pages uses a similar sounding word or syllable from English to describe the sounds. It is good practice to repeat them out loud as you progress through the book.

STROKES & LINES

Japanese scripts are traditionally written with a brush and have an inky, painted look. Even though we use modern pens now, it's important that we learn to write traditionally, with the same movements and **strokes**. Conveniently, Katakana オ *(or 'o')* contains all three stroke types - we have named them based on how they are made and look:

Stop Stroke   *Jump Fade*   *Fade Stroke*

The "**stop stroke**" is exactly how it sounds, where you bring the line to a definite stop before lifting your pen. The "**jump fade**" is made with a quick flick of the pen from the paper at the end of that stroke. The "**fade stroke**" is made by lifting your pen more gently from the paper while your hand is still in motion. You can imagine how the line might get thinner and fade out if you were gradually lifting a thicker brush tip from the page.

Compared to Hiragana, with their round and curved shapes, **Katakana** are drawn with more of the "**stop**" and "**fade**" strokes with far fewer "**jump fade**" marks.

WRITING STYLES

This book will teach you how to write Katakana with the standard movements based on brushed appearances, but you will encounter other styles as you learn:

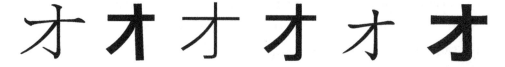

These characters all have the same meaning but look a little different because they are made either by hand, with pens or pencils, or displayed as a modern digital font on a screen or in print. Even though the appearance changes slightly, the meaning remains.

Part 2

LEARN HOW TO WRITE KATAKANA

ア　ア　**a**

SPEAK　Pronounced like the 'a' in car or father, but shorter.

LEARN　This kana is drawn with two fade strokes.

The first stroke starts as a horizontal line from the left before making a sharp turn back in and down to centre. Start your second stroke at the end of the first, curving your pen down and to the left. The second stroke fades out as it approaches the bottom left of the cell.

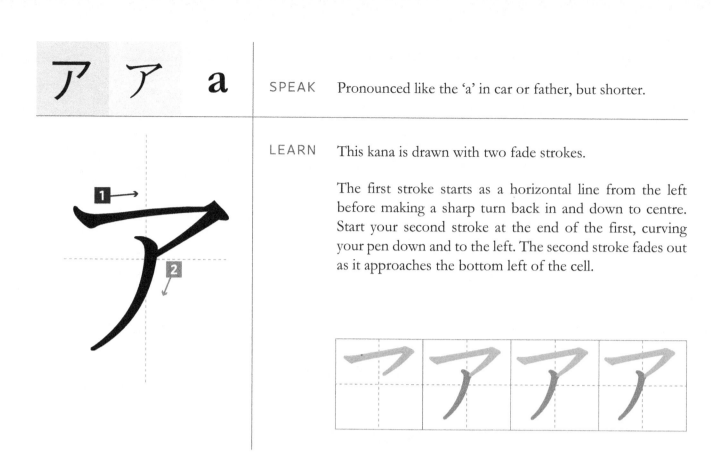

WRITE

First, draw this character in the large cells below

14

ア ア

ラ ラ

イ　イ　　i

Pronounced like the 'ee' in eel.

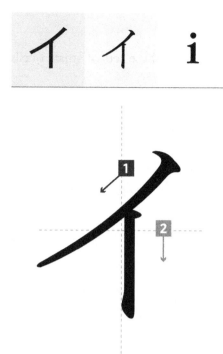

LEARN　This kana is drawn with two strokes; a fade and a stop.

Your first mark is a slightly curved diagonal line, beginning high in the upper right of the cell, and fading out in the bottom left. The next stroke starts around the centre of your first stroke, just to the right of the middle, moving straight down to a stop near the bottom.

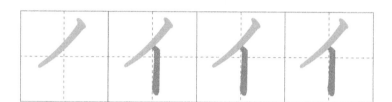

WRITE

First, draw this character in the large cells below

Now practice in these sets of smaller cells

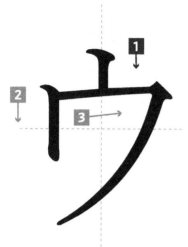 ウ ウ **u**

SPEAK   Pronounced like the 'oo' in zoo.

LEARN   This kana is drawn with three strokes; stop, stop, fade.

Make the first vertical mark with a short stop stroke in the upper middle area. The second short stop mark is another vertical line to the left of the first one, and a little lower down. Your final mark begins where your second started. Moving your pen horizontally from left to right, touch the end of the first stroke and then, at the right of the cell, make a sharp turn down and left in a fading curve.

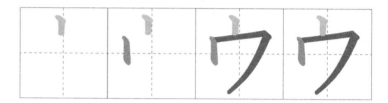

WRITE

First, draw this character in the large cells below

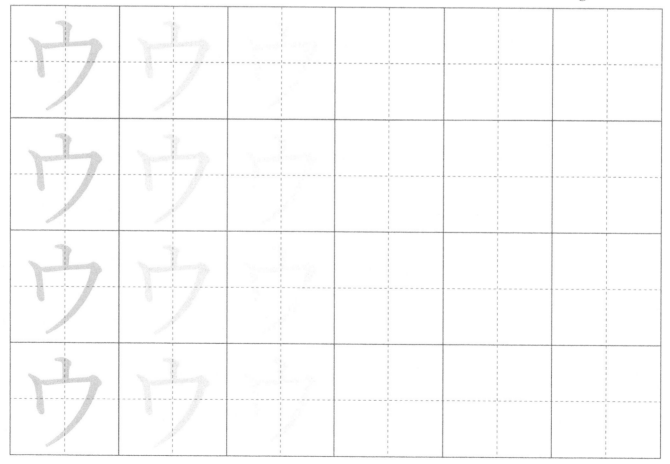

18

PRACTICE

ウ ウ

ウ ウ

エ エ e

LEARN   This kana is drawn with three strokes; all stops.

Start with the horizontal line across the middle in the upper part of the cell. Your second mark then starts in the middle of the first, drawn down the center line. The final stroke is another horizontal line, from left to right, that passes across the end of the second mark at the center. To make sure your writing has good balance, your final mark should be wider than the first one.

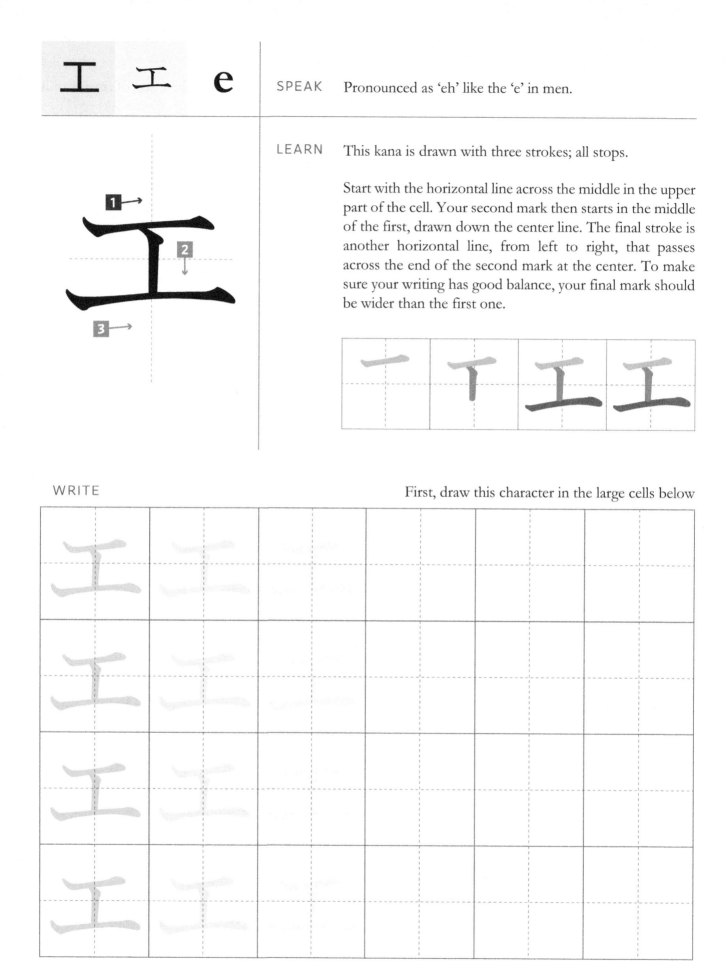

WRITE   First, draw this character in the large cells below

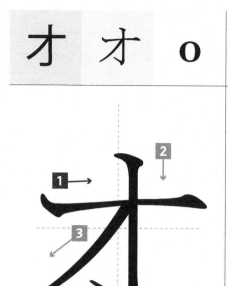

オ オ **o**

LEARN   This kana has three strokes; stop, jump fade, and fade.

Start by drawing a long horizontal line from left to right. Your second stroke is a vertical line that intersects with the first around one third of the way from the right side. Finish the second stroke by flicking your pen from the page (this is called a hane). Your final stroke starts at the intersection of strokes 1 and 2, and curves down and left with a fade - it should not extend lower than the second stroke.

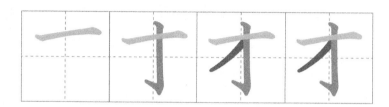

WRITE   First, draw this character in the large cells below

Now practice in these sets of smaller cells

才 才

才 才

カ カ **ka**

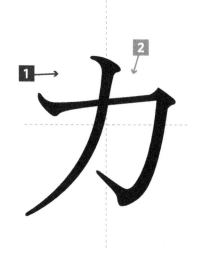

LEARN   This kana is drawn with two strokes; jump fade, stop.

This is an angular version of hiragana か and starts with a slightly inclined horizontal line that turns downwards sharply. The downwards part should have a slight curve backwards and diagonally left. End this stroke with a hane by flicking your pen from the paper. Your second stroke is diagonal line down, with a curve to the left and up.

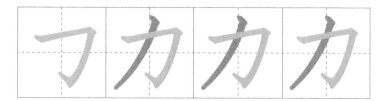

WRITE   First, draw this character in the large cells below

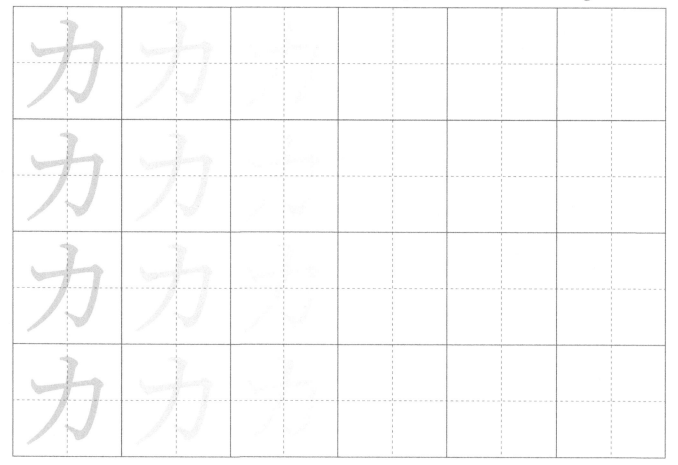

Now practice in these sets of smaller cells

カ カ

カ カ

 **ki**

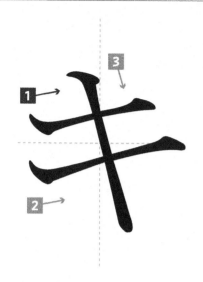

LEARN   Drawn with three strokes; stop, stop, and stop.

You will notice that this Katakana is also very similar to the Hiragana counterpart - strokes 1 and 2 are parallel diagonal lines from left to right, in an upwards direction, the second slightly longer than the first. Your final mark is simply another straight diagonal line, from upper left to lower right. It should cut roughly through the middles of your first two strokes.

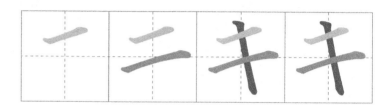

WRITE

First, draw this character in the large cells below

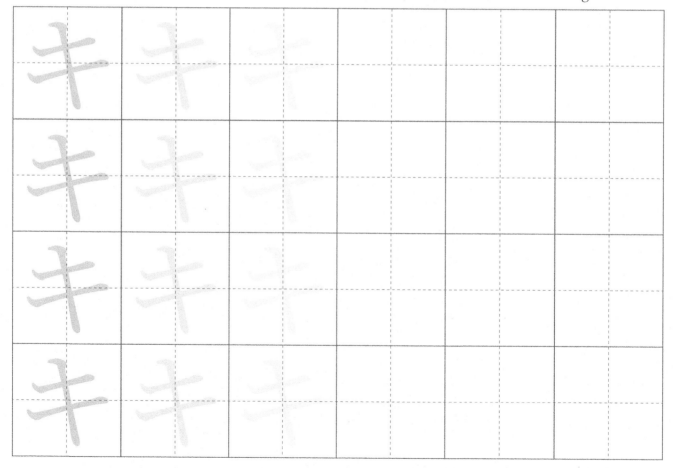

26

ク ク ku

Pronounced like the 'koo' in cuckoo.

LEARN   This kana is drawn with two strokes; both fades.

Start with the first curved diagonal line from the upper middle, down and to the left. Start your second stroke in roughly the same place as your first. It's begins with a much shorter horizontal mark than previous kana, before a sharp turn and into another much longer diagonal curve down and left. Practice making the two diagonal parts run in parallel to one another for extra neat writing!

WRITE

First, draw this character in the large cells below

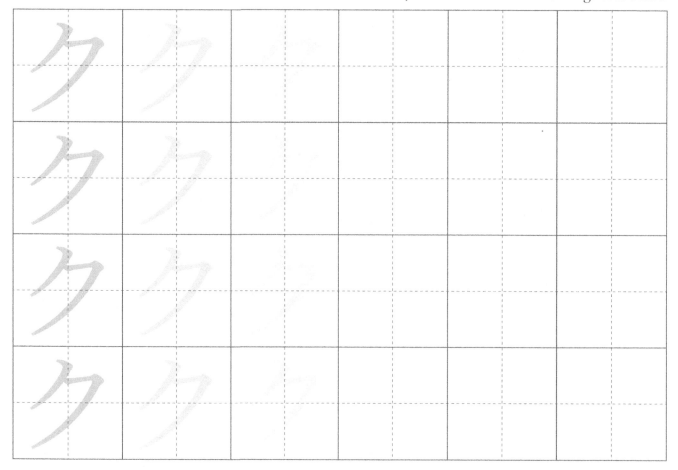

28

ㄅㄅ
ㄅㄅ

ケ ケ **ke**

Pronounced like the 'ke' in Kenneth

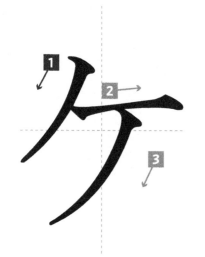

LEARN   This kana has three strokes: fade, stop, fade.

Starting in a similar way to the previous katakana ク, draw the first diagonal line and end with a fade by reducing the pressure and gently lifting your pen. The second mark starts from the middle of your first line this time, and is just a longer horizontal line that stops. Begin the third stroke at the midpoint of the second line, and move your pen in a curve down and to the left with a fade - parallel to the first.

WRITE   First, draw this character in the large cells below

Now practice in these sets of smaller cells

コ コ **ko**

SPEAK Pronounced like the 'co' in core

LEARN This kana is drawn with two strokes: both stops.

The first mark is a horizontal line that stops and turns downwards quite sharply. Your second mark is another horizontal stroke from the left, and should meet the end of your first stroke with a stop. The two horizontal parts should be parallel and the same length.

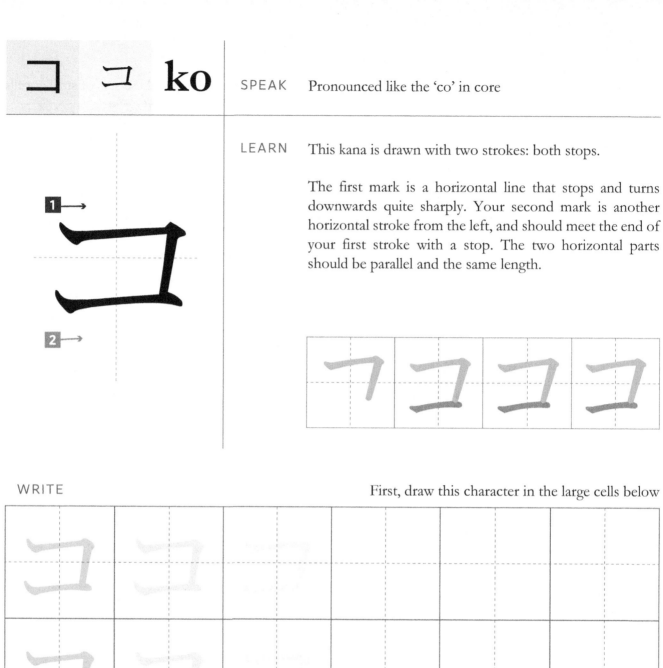

WRITE First, draw this character in the large cells below

Now practice in these sets of smaller cells

サ サ **sa**

Pronounced like the 'sa' in sardines.

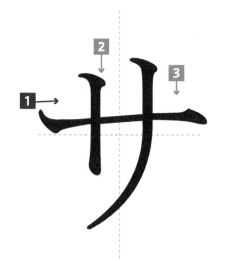

LEARN   This kana is drawn with three strokes: stop, stop, fade.

Start this kana with a long horizontal line. Your second line cuts through the first one roughly one third from the left, drawn straight down to a stop. The third stroke is a longer curved line that cuts through the first, roughly one third of the length across from the right. It starts as a vertical line before the intersection but curves left after crossing down through your first stroke.

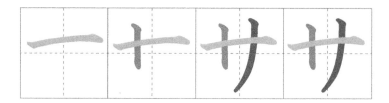

WRITE   First, draw this character in the large cells below

Now practice in these sets of smaller cells

サ サ
サ サ

 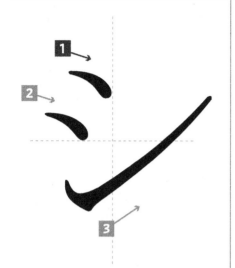 **shi**

SPEAK Pronounced like 'she' as in sheet.

LEARN Draw this kana with three strokes; stop, stop, fade.

Both the first and second strokes are short stop marks, made in parallel and at a slight angle down. Your third stroke begins in the lower left area, below the first strokes, and curves up and to the right. You should pay special attention to the spacing of the three strokes and the points that they start from. We will see some very similar looking characters further ahead.

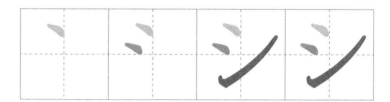

WRITE   First, draw this character in the large cells below

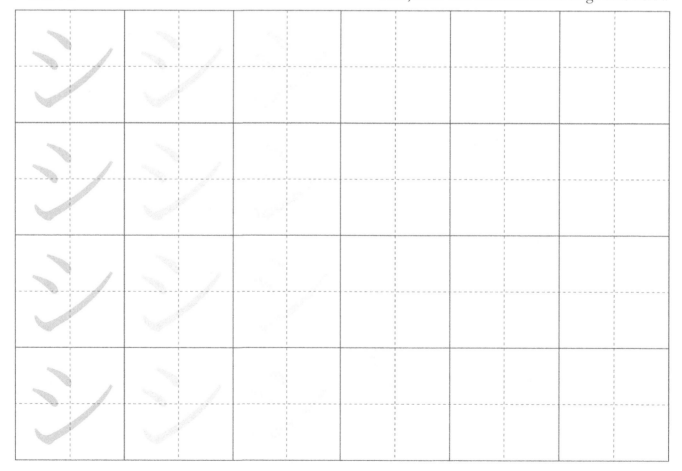

ス ス **su**

SPEAK   Pronounced like the 'su' in super

LEARN   This has two strokes; a long fade, and a stop.

This character begins with a stroke that we have made in earlier kana. It starts with a horizontal line from left to right before that sharp turn into a curve, moving down and back to the left in a fade. Your second mark is a relatively short stop stroke, and starts from around the midpoint of your curve from the first stroke.

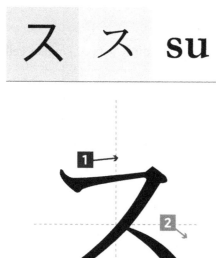

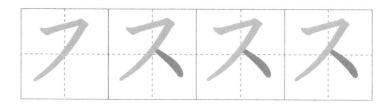

WRITE   First, draw this character in the large cells below

Now practice in these sets of smaller cells

セ セ **se**

Pronounced like 'say' but with less 'y'.

LEARN This kana is drawn with two strokes; a fade and a stop.

Begin the first stroke with a relatively long, inclined line from left to right. As you approach the right side, it turns into a short fade down and to the left - but not quite as sharply as other kana. Your second mark begins as a straight vertical line, drawn from the top and then gently sweeping to the right, near the bottom of the cell.

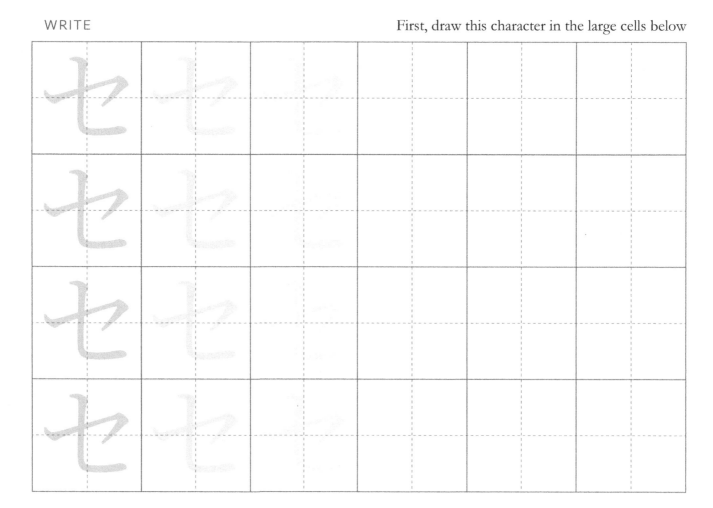

WRITE

First, draw this character in the large cells below

Now practice in these sets of smaller cells

せ せ

ち ち

ソ ソ **so**

SPEAK Pronounced like the 'so' in soy.

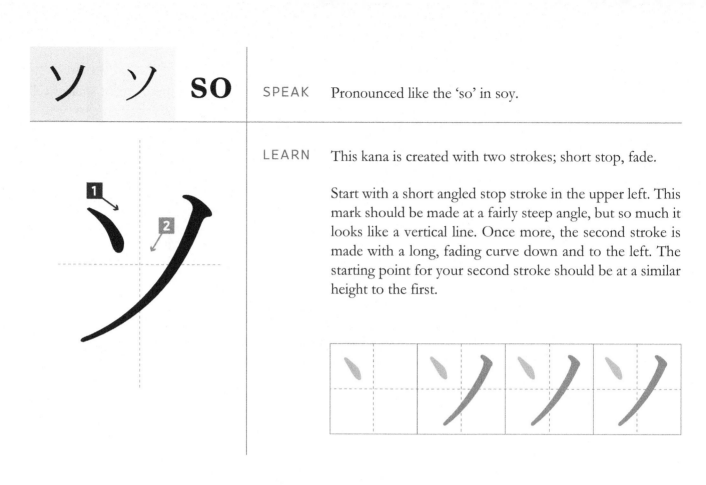

LEARN This kana is created with two strokes; short stop, fade.

Start with a short angled stop stroke in the upper left. This mark should be made at a fairly steep angle, but so much it looks like a vertical line. Once more, the second stroke is made with a long, fading curve down and to the left. The starting point for your second stroke should be at a similar height to the first.

WRITE

First, draw this character in the large cells below

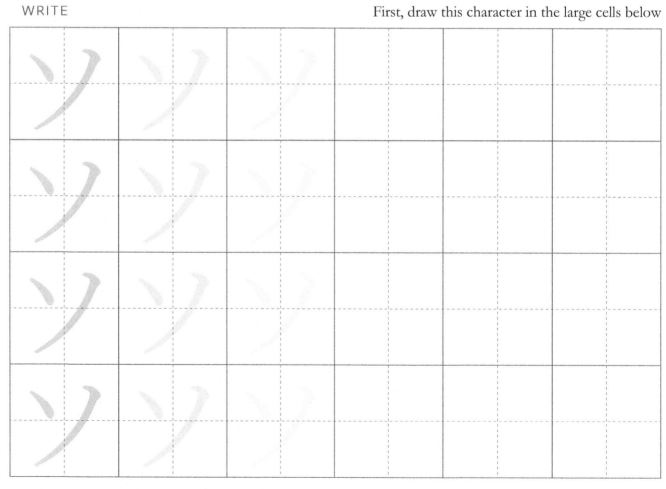

ツ ツ

ソ ソ

タ タ **ta**

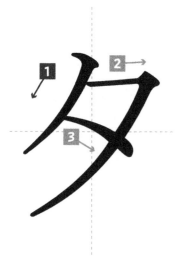

LEARN   This kana is drawn with three strokes; fade, fade, stop.

Another kana with some now familiar shapes. In a similar way to ク and ケ, your first stroke is a fading diagonal curve from upper center to lower left. The second stroke begins with a horizontal line from the same start point as the first, curving down to the left. Your last mark is a short diagonal line from the middle of the first stroke. It cuts across the middle of the second stroke.

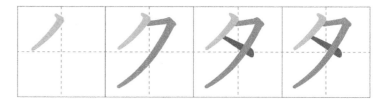

WRITE   First, draw this character in the large cells below

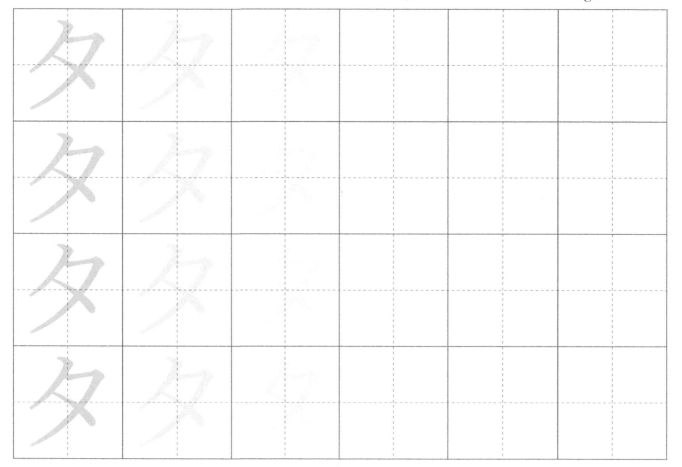

Now practice in these sets of smaller cells

チ チ **chi**

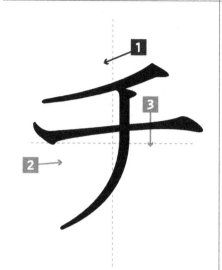

Pronounced just like the 'chi' in tai-chi.

LEARN This kana is drawn with three strokes; fade, stop, fade.

Your first line is a shallow, fading curve from the upper right and down slightly to the left side. Stroke number 2 is a long horizontal line with a stop. Your third stroke should begin in the middle of the first curve and intersect with the second stroke, before curving down and to the left. Make sure that your second line is wider than the first stroke on both sides!

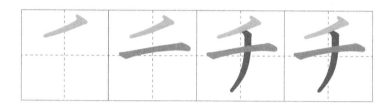

WRITE

First, draw this character in the large cells below

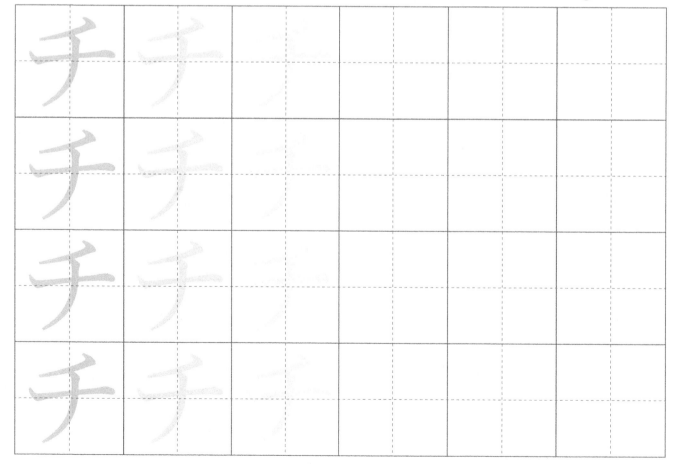

手 手

 **ツ** ツ **tsu**

SPEAK | Pronounced just as the 'tsu' in tsunami, with a silent 't'.

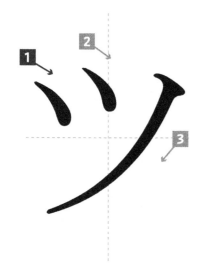

LEARN | This kana has three strokes; two stops, and a fade.

This character looks similar to the Katakana シ and both the first two strokes are once again made as two parallel, angled lines. Your third line is a sweeping, fading curve down to the left from the upper right. For the same reasons, take care with the spacing of your start points for each stroke.

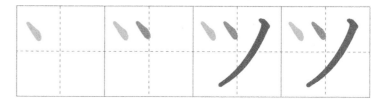

WRITE

First, draw this character in the large cells below

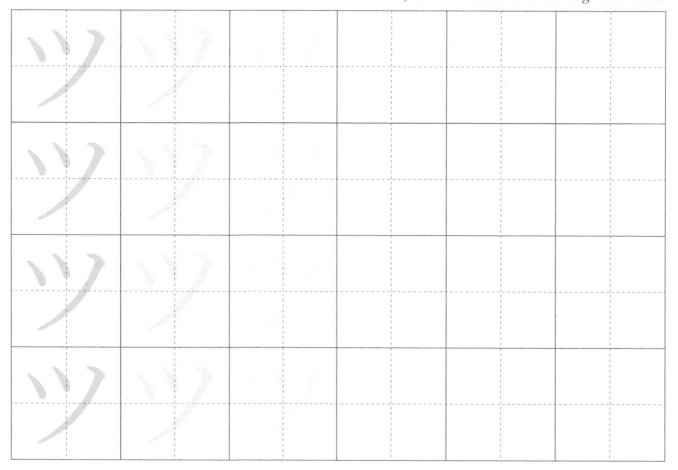

Now practice in these sets of smaller cells

テ テ **te**

Pronounced like the 'te' in ten.

This kana is drawn with three strokes; stop, stop, fade.

This kana starts with two parallel stop strokes, making horizontal lines from left to right. Make sure that your second line is longer than the first. Your third mark is a shorter, curved diagonal line down and to the left side. It starts at the midpoint of your second stroke.

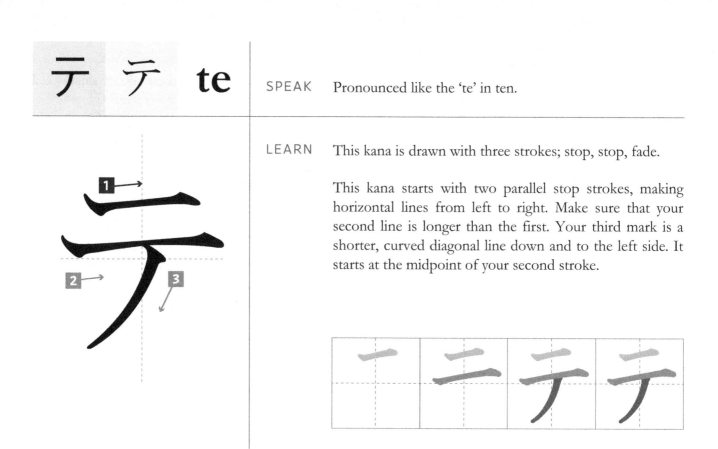

WRITE   First, draw this character in the large cells below

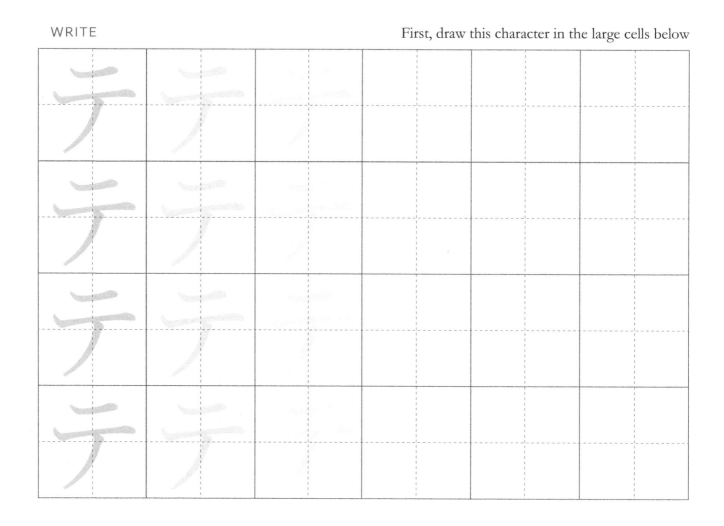

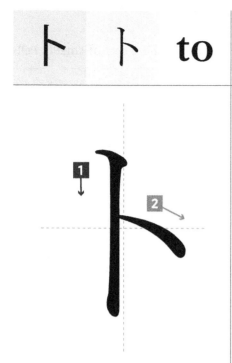 ト　ト　**to**

Pronounced like the 'to' in tick-tock.

LEARN This kana is created with two strokes; stop, stop.

Draw a long vertical line starting near the top of the cell, and slightly left of center, ending with a stop near the bottom of the cell. Your second line is a much shorter stop mark, starting above the center of the cell, and moving down and right in a diagonal direction.

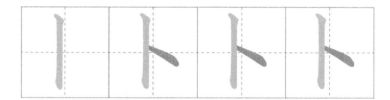

WRITE First, draw this character in the large cells below

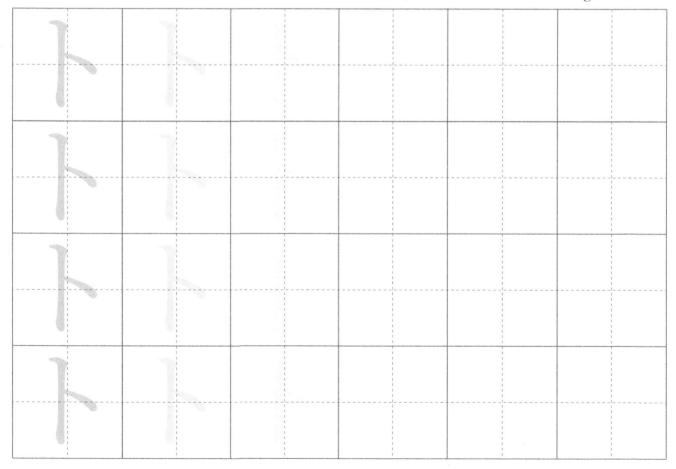

52

Now practice in these sets of smaller cells

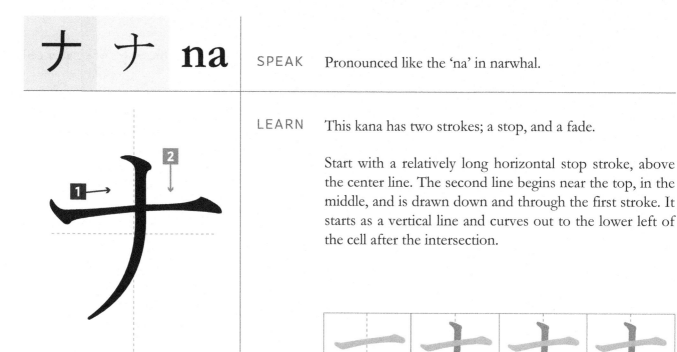

ナ ナ **na**

SPEAK   Pronounced like the 'na' in narwhal.

LEARN   This kana has two strokes; a stop, and a fade.

Start with a relatively long horizontal stop stroke, above the center line. The second line begins near the top, in the middle, and is drawn down and through the first stroke. It starts as a vertical line and curves out to the lower left of the cell after the intersection.

WRITE   First, draw this character in the large cells below

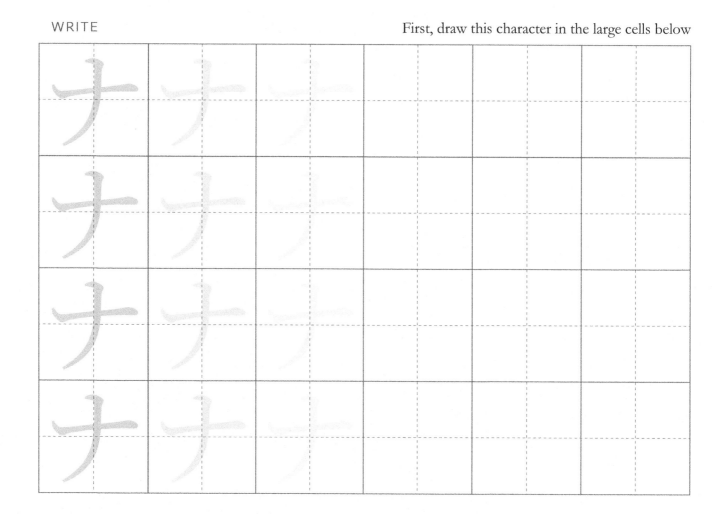

二 二 ni

Pronounced like the 'nee' in needle, but shorter.

LEARN   This kana has two strokes; both are stops.

As one of the more simple of the Katakana symbols, we draw 二 with two parallel lines. Each moves horizontally from left to right, with a slight incline. Your second stroke should be longer than your first, extending on both sides.

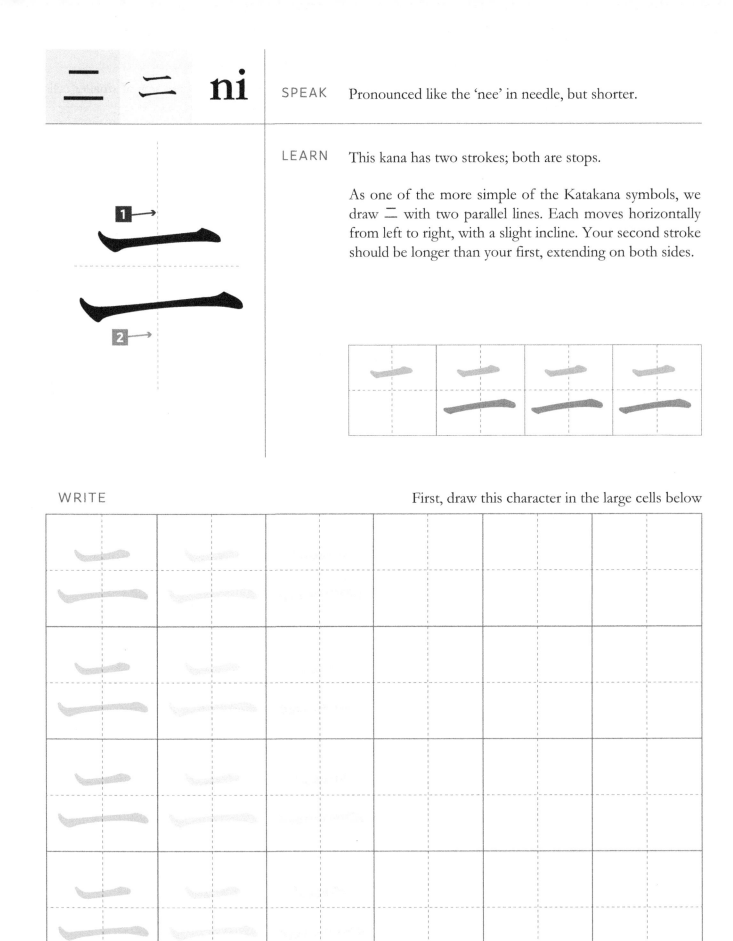

WRITE

First, draw this character in the large cells below

Now practice in these sets of smaller cells

ヌ　ヌ　**nu**

SPEAK Pronounced like the 'noo' in noodles but short.

LEARN Drawn with two strokes; a long fade, stop.

Begin your first stroke with a slightly inclined horizontal line from left to right and up just a little. Without lifting the pen, make a sharp turn down into a long sweeping curve. It ends as a fade in the bottom left part of the cell. Your second mark is a shorter curve that ends with a stop. It begins below the start of your first stroke and cuts through the middle of the curve you just made.

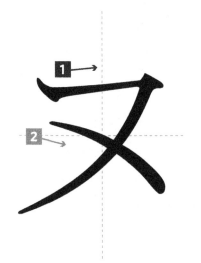

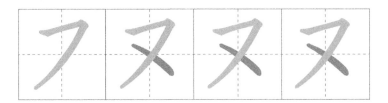

WRITE   First, draw this character in the large cells below

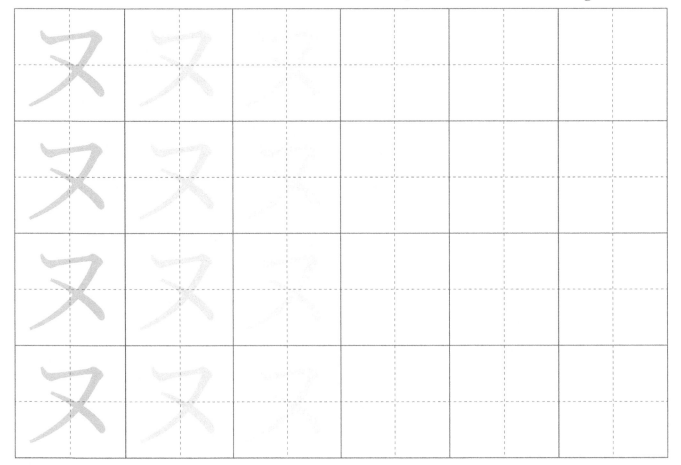

PRACTICE

Now practice in these sets of smaller cells

叉 叉
叉 叉

59

ネ ネ **ne**

Pronounced like the 'ne' in nest.

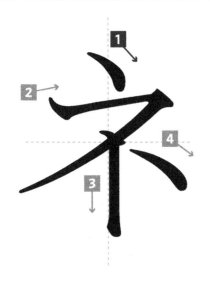

LEARN This kana has four strokes; stop, fade, stop and stop.

Begin with a short angled stop mark in the upper center. Your second mark starts with a horizontal line before a sharp turn into a fading curve down and left. Stroke three is a vertical line with a stop, starting in the middle of the curve in stroke 2. The final mark is a short diagonal line that should be roughly the same length as the lower end of your long curve.

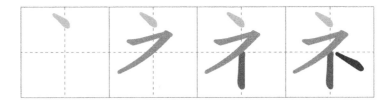

WRITE   First, draw this character in the large cells below

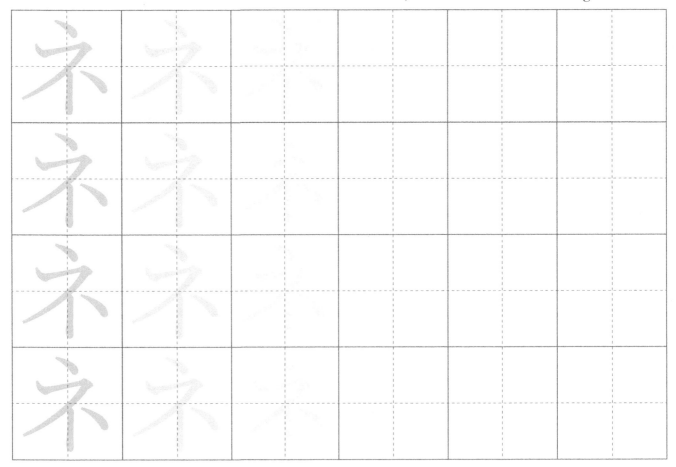

60

森 森

森 森

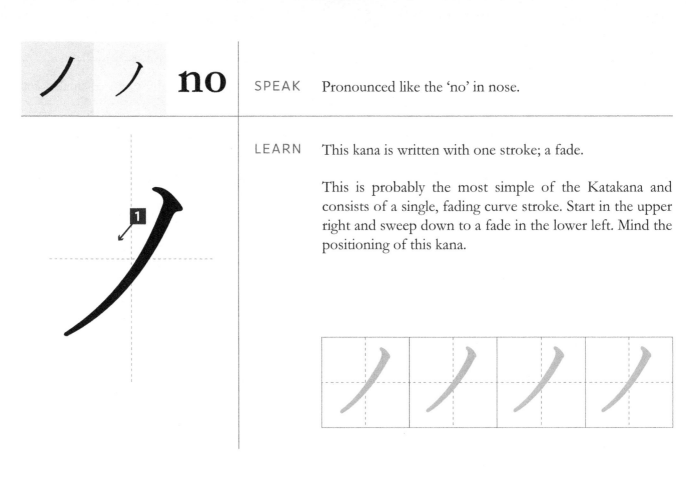

ノ ノ **no**

Pronounced like the 'no' in nose.

LEARN This kana is written with one stroke; a fade.

This is probably the most simple of the Katakana and consists of a single, fading curve stroke. Start in the upper right and sweep down to a fade in the lower left. Mind the positioning of this kana.

WRITE   First, draw this character in the large cells below

PRACTICE

Now practice in these sets of smaller cells

63

ハ ハ **ha**

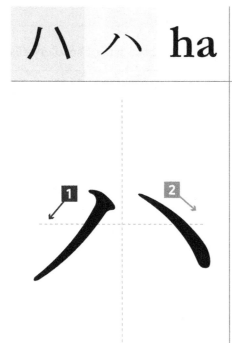

Pronounced as the 'ha' when laughing, like ha-ha.

LEARN Draw this kana with two strokes; a fade and a stop.

Your first stroke is a curved diagonal line from just left of center and fading down to the left. The second mark almost mirrors the first, but ends with a stop in the lower right area. The start points should be spaced apart and positioned away from the center line.

WRITE   First, draw this character in the large cells below

Now practice in these sets of smaller cells

ヒ ヒ hi

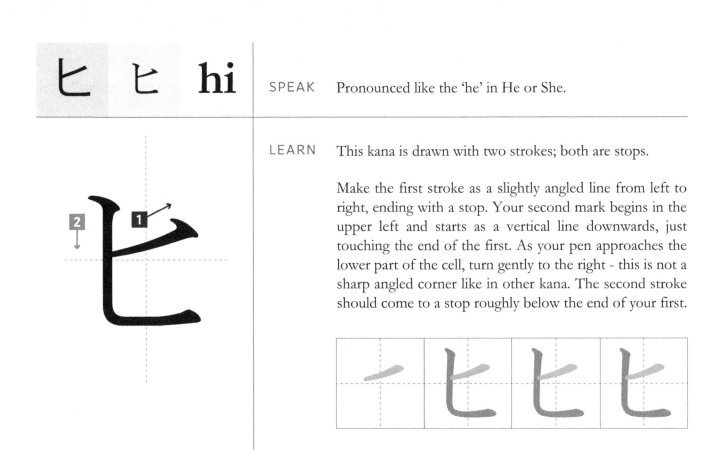

SPEAK   Pronounced like the 'he' in He or She.

LEARN   This kana is drawn with two strokes; both are stops.

Make the first stroke as a slightly angled line from left to right, ending with a stop. Your second mark begins in the upper left and starts as a vertical line downwards, just touching the end of the first. As your pen approaches the lower part of the cell, turn gently to the right - this is not a sharp angled corner like in other kana. The second stroke should come to a stop roughly below the end of your first.

WRITE   First, draw this character in the large cells below

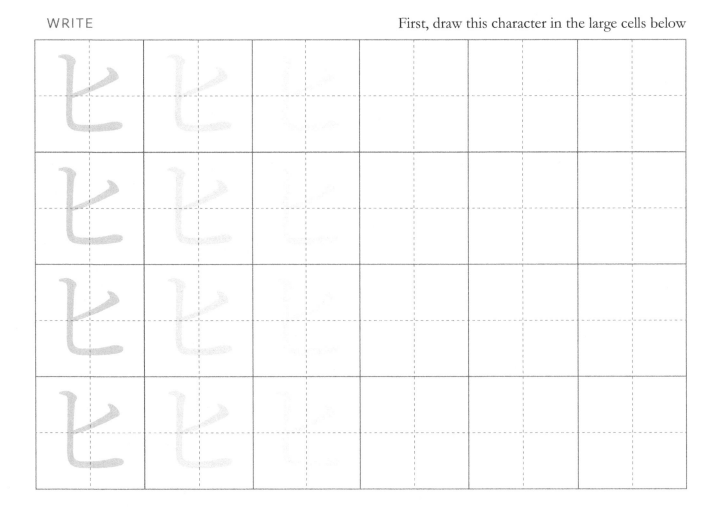

66

PRACTICE

Now practice in these sets of smaller cells

と と

と と

67

フ フ **fu**

SPEAK   Pronounced as 'hu' like the word 'who'.

LEARN   Drawn with a single stroke; it is a long fade.

This kana has been drawn as part of the previous symbols in this workbook. With a shape similar to a *number 7*, it begins with a slightly inclined horizontal line. When your pen approaches the right side of the cell, it should turn quite sharply. Keep your pen on the page as you continue to create the long, fading curve down towards the lower left of the cell.

WRITE   First, draw this character in the large cells below

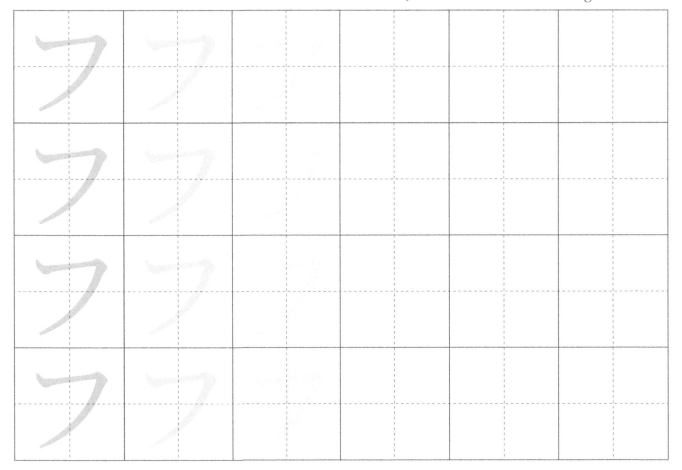

Now practice in these sets of smaller cells

ワ ワ
ラ ラ

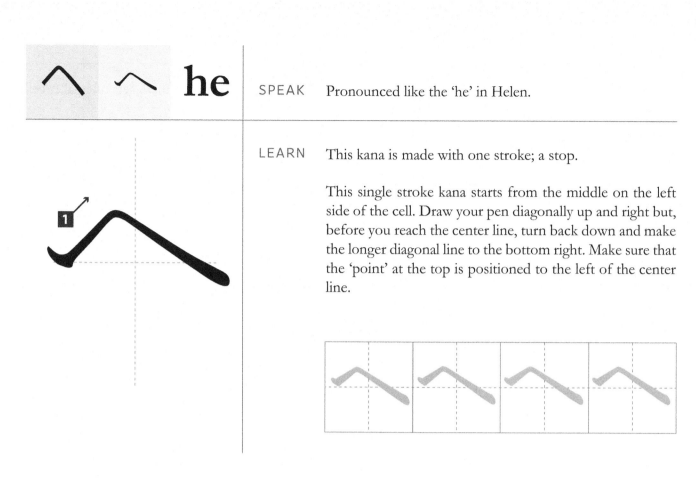

he

Pronounced like the 'he' in Helen.

LEARN   This kana is made with one stroke; a stop.

This single stroke kana starts from the middle on the left side of the cell. Draw your pen diagonally up and right but, before you reach the center line, turn back down and make the longer diagonal line to the bottom right. Make sure that the 'point' at the top is positioned to the left of the center line.

WRITE   First, draw this character in the large cells below

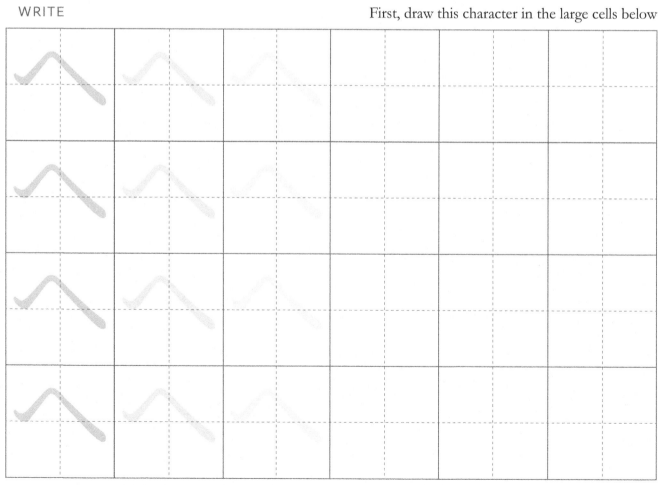

Now practice in these sets of smaller cells

ホ ホ ho

SPEAK   Pronounced like the 'ho' in home.

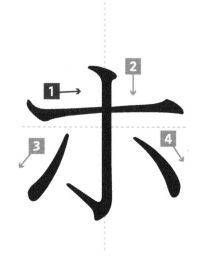

LEARN   This kana has four strokes; stop, jump fade, stop and stop.

The first stroke is a horizontal line from left to right. Your second stroke is a vertical line, cutting across the middle of the first stroke, just above the center of the cell. End with a hane by flicking your pen from the paper. The third and fourth strokes are made in the same way that we draw the kana ハ , mirroring each other. They should not make contact with any of your other marks.

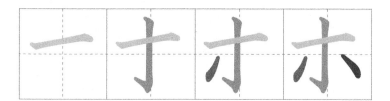

WRITE   First, draw this character in the large cells below

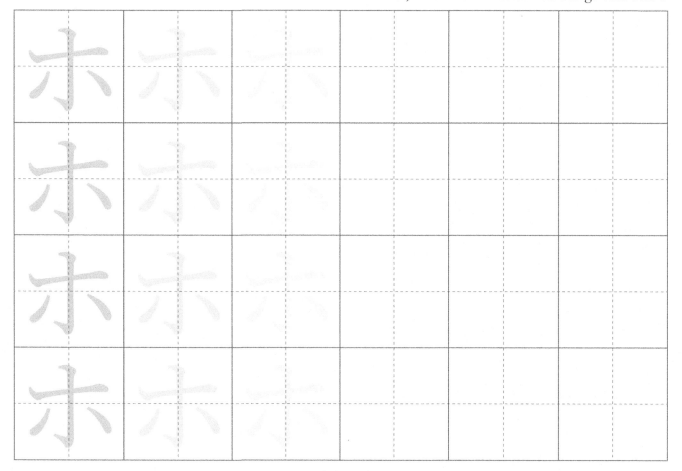

Now practice in these sets of smaller cells

六 木
六 木

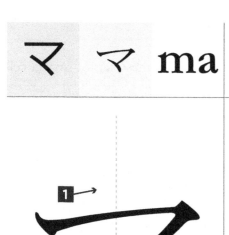 **ma**

Pronounced like the 'ma' in market.

LEARN Drawn with two strokes; long fade, short stop.

Beginning with a familiar first stroke, draw your pen across the cell in a horizontal line. Without lifting your pen, turn sharply back and down with a shorter faded curve to the left. Your second stroke is a relatively short line, made at an angle down and to the right. Take care not to confuse this with the kana ア that we learned at the beginning!

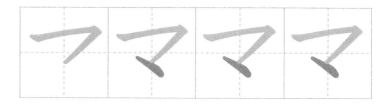

WRITE   First, draw this character in the large cells below

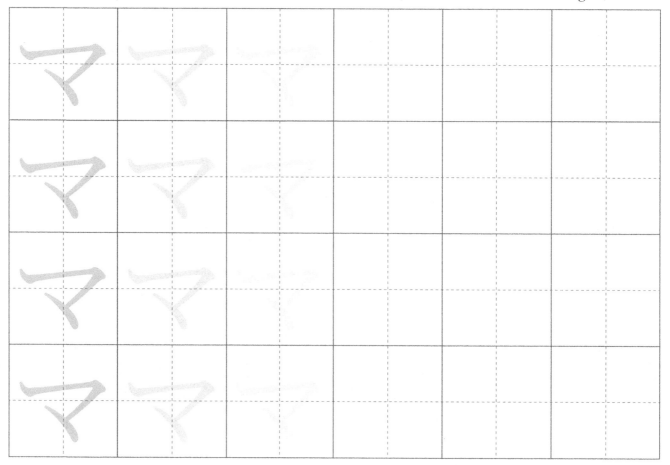

74

Now practice in these sets of smaller cells

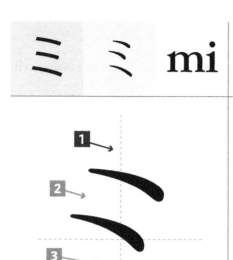 **mi**

Pronounced just like 'me'.

LEARN Drawn with three strokes; each is a short stop.

This kana is relatively simple, consisting of three short, parallel lines. Each is drawn at a slight angle, bringing your pen to a stop as you move down from left to right. The third stroke is ever so slightly longer, and the start position just a little to the right.

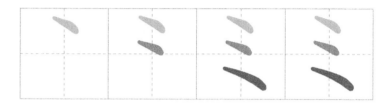

WRITE First, draw this character in the large cells below

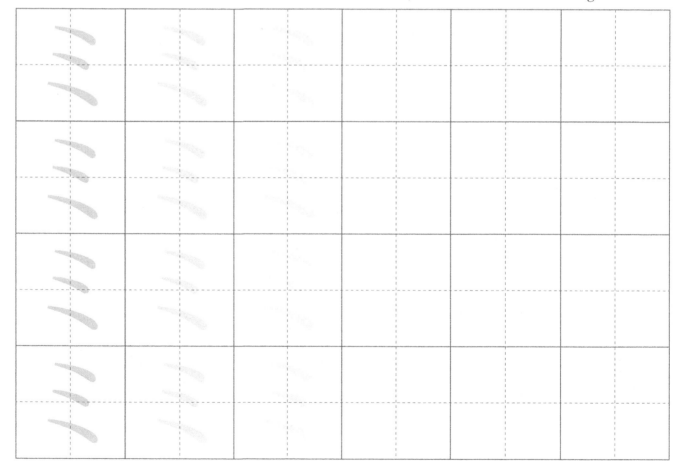

76

Now practice in these sets of smaller cells

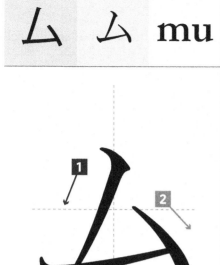 ム mu

Pronounced like 'moo' but in move.

LEARN Draw this kana with two strokes; stop and stop.

It almost looks like three separate strokes, but the first creates a sort of L-shape. Begin with a straight line, drawn diagonally from the upper middle to the lower left. Keep your pen on the paper and make a sharp turn to the right. Move across the cell at a much more shallow angle and end with a stop. The second line is a short diagonal stop mark that should touch the end of the first stroke as it descends.

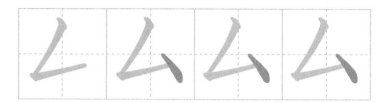

WRITE

First, draw this character in the large cells below

Now practice in these sets of smaller cells

 **me**

Pronounced as 'meh' like the 'me' in mend.

LEARN This kana is drawn with two strokes; a fade and a stop.

Your first stroke is a relatively long curved line, drawn from the upper right quadrant to the lower left. This line should end with a fade. The second diagonal mark is a shorter curve that cuts across the middle of your first stroke and ends with a stop.

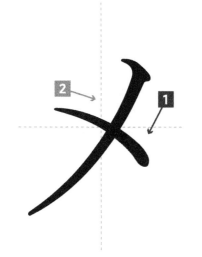

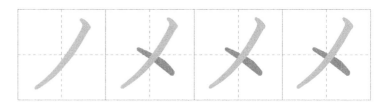

WRITE   First, draw this character in the large cells below

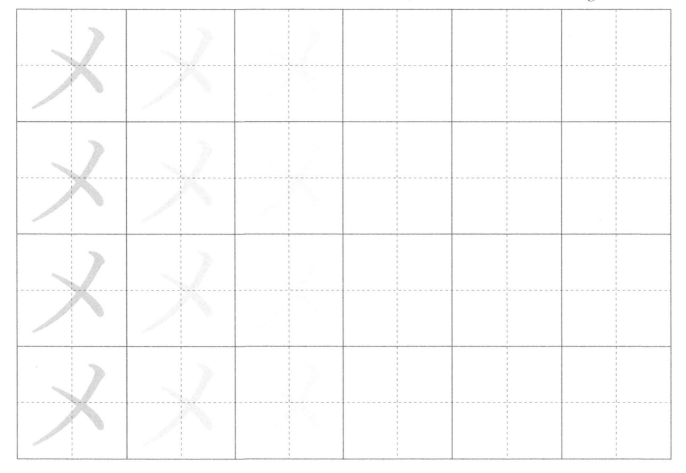

Now practice in these sets of smaller cells

 モ モ **mo**

Pronounced just like the 'mo' in more.

LEARN

This kana has three strokes; all of them are stops.

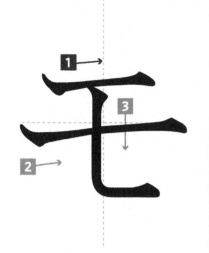

Start this kana by drawing the first and second strokes as two horizontal lines. The second should be a little longer than the first. Your third stroke begins on the first stroke and is drawn as a vertical line downwards, to begin with. It will cut through your second stroke and, as your pen approaches the bottom of the cell, turn gently to the right and across to a stop on the right.

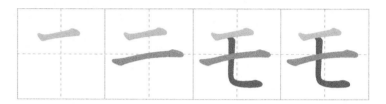

WRITE

First, draw this character in the large cells below

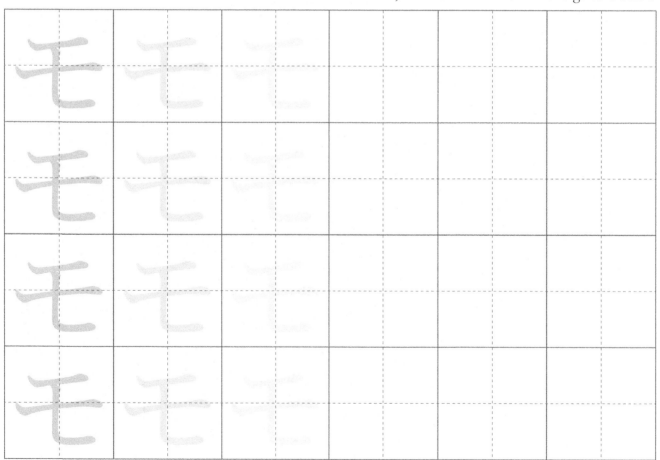

Now practice in these sets of smaller cells

 **ya**

Pronounced like the 'ya' in yard'

LEARN   Draw this kana with two strokes; a fade and a stop.

We begin drawing this kana with a straight line from left to right, at a relatively shallow angle up. As we approach the right side of the cell, it turns sharply down and back in towards the center with a short fade. Your second stroke is a long diagonal line from the upper left part of the cell, closer to the center than the side, and it cuts through the first stroke roughly one third of the way from the start.

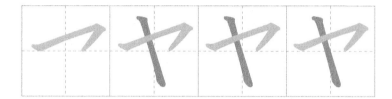

WRITE   First, draw this character in the large cells below

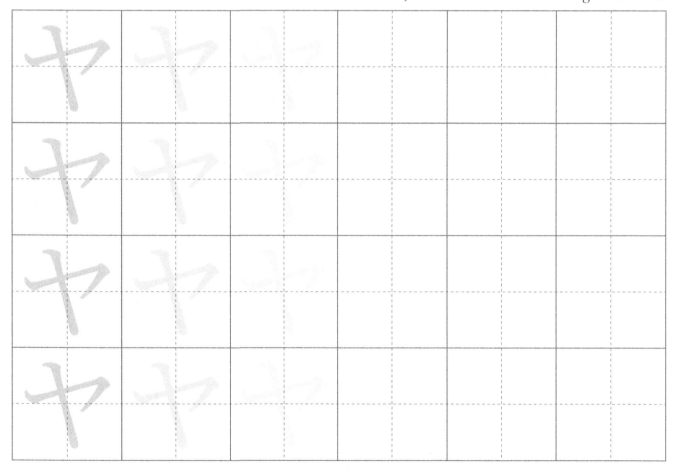

Now practice in these sets of smaller cells

ヤ ヤ

ユ ユ yu

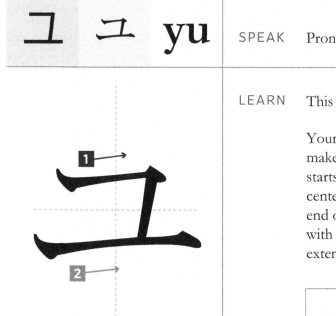

LEARN This kana is drawn with two strokes; both are stops.

Your first stroke begins as a short horizontal line and then makes a sharp turn down to a stop. Your second mark starts further to the left side than your first, and below the center line. It is a longer horizontal line and must touch the end of the first stroke. So that this symbol is not confused with katakana ⊐, take care to make the second stroke extend further on both sides.

WRITE   First, draw this character in the large cells below

86

Now practice in these sets of smaller cells

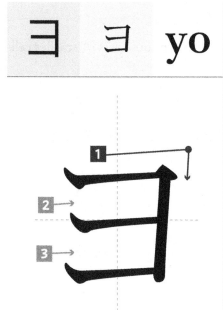 ヨ **yo**

LEARN   This kana is drawn with three strokes; all stops.

This kana looks like is a backwards letter E and, similar to the kana, on the previous page, starts with a horizontal line that turns into a vertical line on the right side. Your second line is slightly shorter, drawn across the middle of the cell to meet the center of the vertical line. Finally, the third line is a slightly longer one, from left to right, that meets the end of the first stroke in the lower right quadrant.

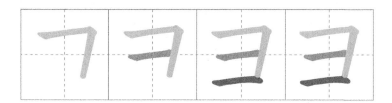

WRITE   First, draw this character in the large cells below

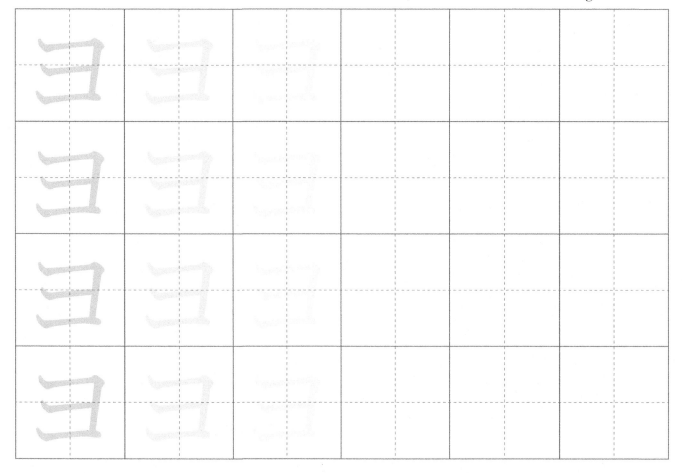

ㅋ ㅋ

ㅋ ㅋ

ラ ラ **ra**

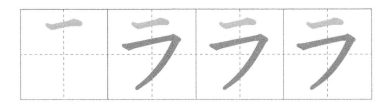

SPEAK   Pronounced like the 'ra' in ramen.

LEARN   This kana is drawn with two strokes; stop, fade.

Begin by making a short horizontal line with a stop stroke near the top of the cell. Stroke number two is like the *number 7 shape*, and starts with a longer, horizontal line in parallel to the first stroke. It then turns to make a long, curved diagonal line. Fade this stroke out towards the central area at the bottom.

WRITE   First, draw this character in the large cells below

PRACTICE

Now practice in these sets of smaller cells

ラ ラ
ヲ ヲ

91

リ リ ri

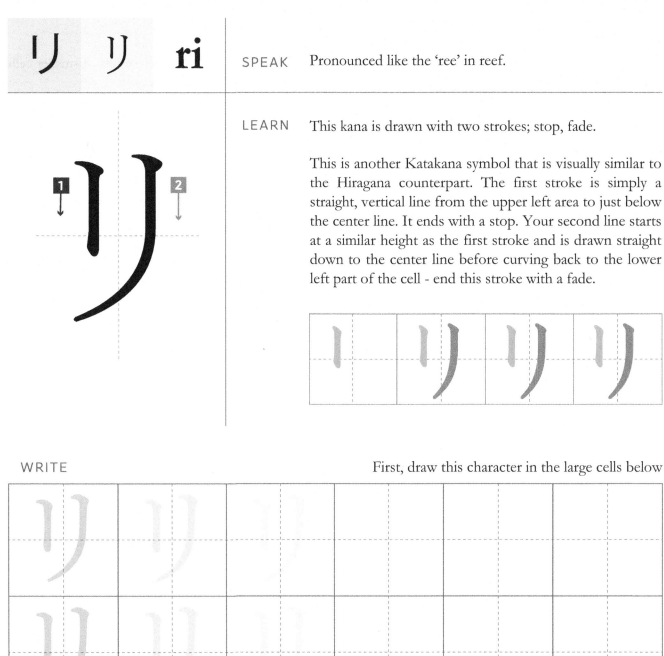

LEARN   This kana is drawn with two strokes; stop, fade.

This is another Katakana symbol that is visually similar to the Hiragana counterpart. The first stroke is simply a straight, vertical line from the upper left area to just below the center line. It ends with a stop. Your second line starts at a similar height as the first stroke and is drawn straight down to the center line before curving back to the lower left part of the cell - end this stroke with a fade.

WRITE   First, draw this character in the large cells below

Now practice in these sets of smaller cells

リ リ

リ リ

リ

リ

ル ル **ru**

SPEAK   Pronounced like the 'rew' in brew.

LEARN   This kana is drawn with two strokes; both are fades.

Begin with a curved line from the upper area down to the lower left side and finish it with a fade. The second stroke begins as a straight vertical line from higher point than the first, and just to the right of the center line. As your pen approaches the bottom, turn sharply to the right and up with a slightly curved, fading stroke to end.

WRITE   First, draw this character in the large cells below

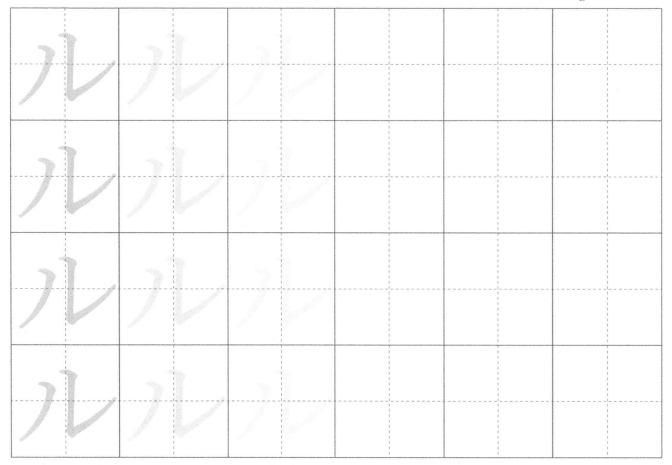

94

Now practice in these sets of smaller cells

ル ル ル

ル ル

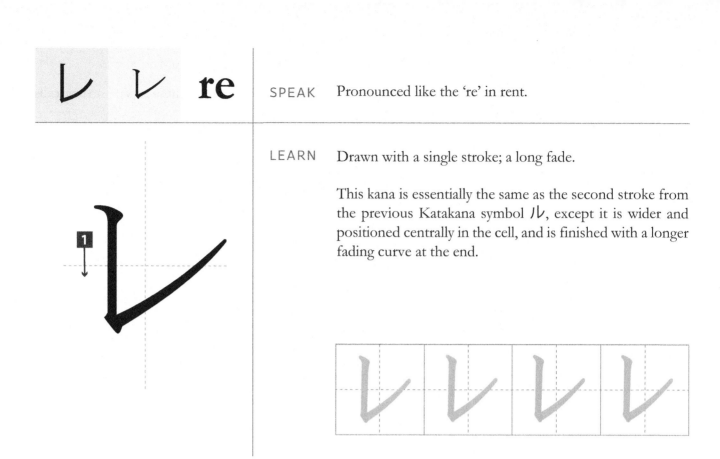

レ レ **re**

LEARN

Drawn with a single stroke; a long fade.

This kana is essentially the same as the second stroke from the previous Katakana symbol ル, except it is wider and positioned centrally in the cell, and is finished with a longer fading curve at the end.

WRITE

First, draw this character in the large cells below

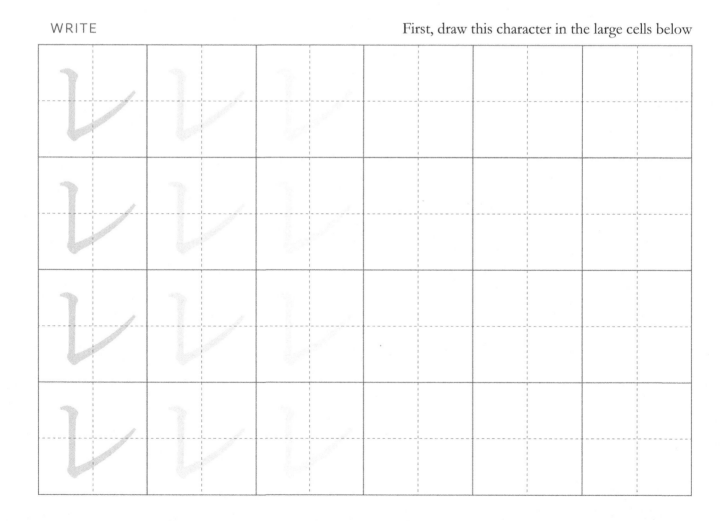

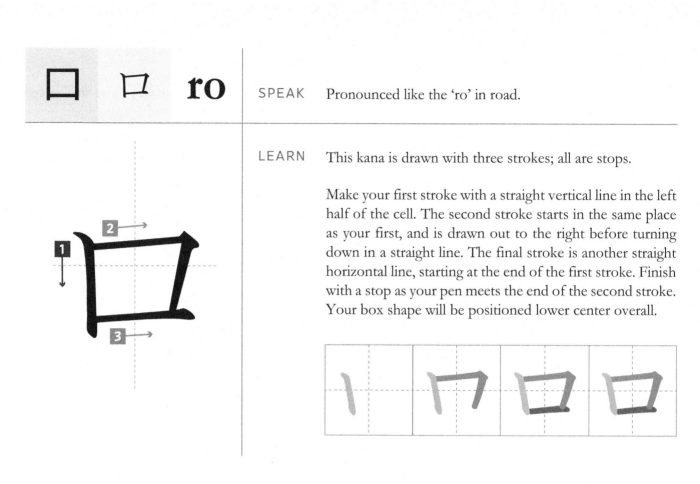

□ □ **ro**

LEARN   This kana is drawn with three strokes; all are stops.

Make your first stroke with a straight vertical line in the left half of the cell. The second stroke starts in the same place as your first, and is drawn out to the right before turning down in a straight line. The final stroke is another straight horizontal line, starting at the end of the first stroke. Finish with a stop as your pen meets the end of the second stroke. Your box shape will be positioned lower center overall.

WRITE   First, draw this character in the large cells below

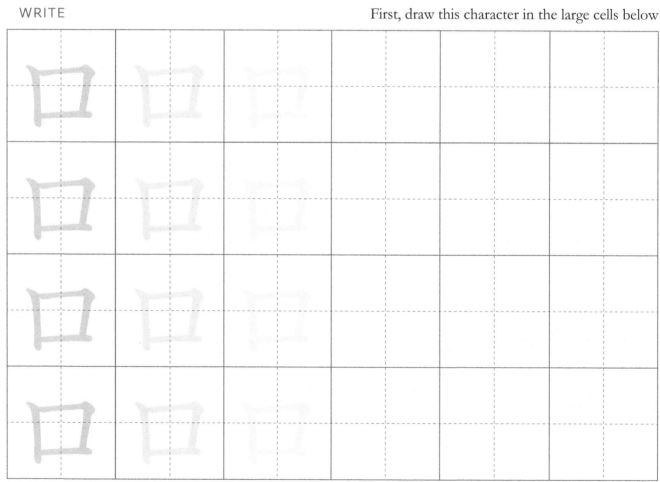

ワ ワ **wa**

SPEAK   Pronounced like the 'wa' in wagon.

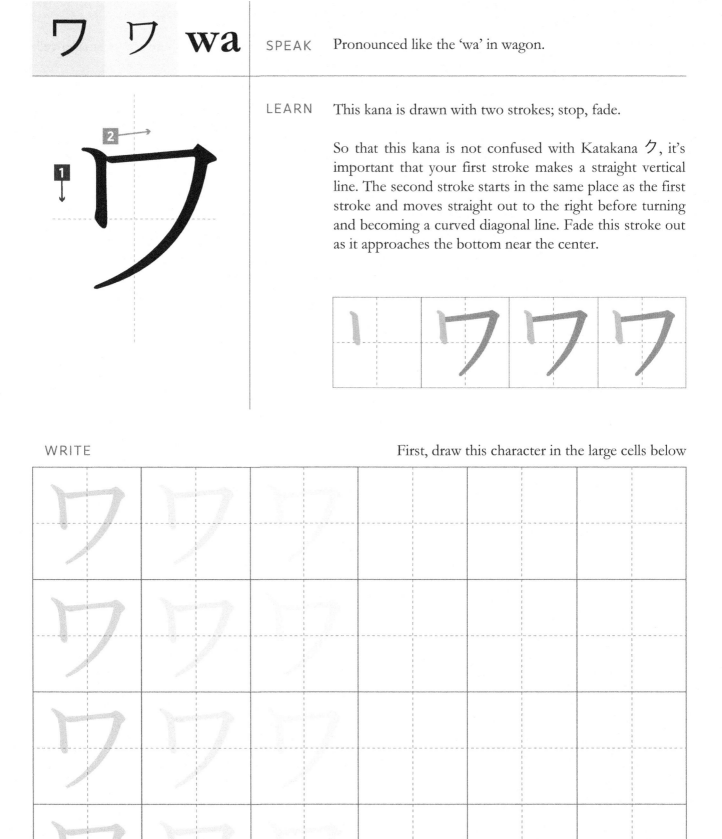

LEARN   This kana is drawn with two strokes; stop, fade.

So that this kana is not confused with Katakana ク, it's important that your first stroke makes a straight vertical line. The second stroke starts in the same place as the first stroke and moves straight out to the right before turning and becoming a curved diagonal line. Fade this stroke out as it approaches the bottom near the center.

WRITE   First, draw this character in the large cells below

100

Now practice in these sets of smaller cells

ワ ワ
ワ ワ

ワ ワ
ワ ワ

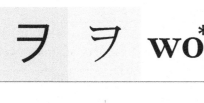 **ヲ ヲ wo***

Pronounced like the 'oh' in woah, with a silent 'w'.

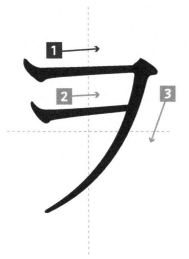

LEARN   Drawn with three strokes; long fade and two stops.

Our penultimate kana symbol starts with two horizontal strokes in the upper half of the cell. They are parallel lines and the second is slightly shorter. The third stroke is a long, sweeping curve that starts at the end of the first stroke. It should meet the end of the second stroke and fade out in the lower left area of the cell.

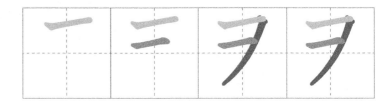

* Uncommon kana, used as a particle.

WRITE   First, draw this character in the large cells below

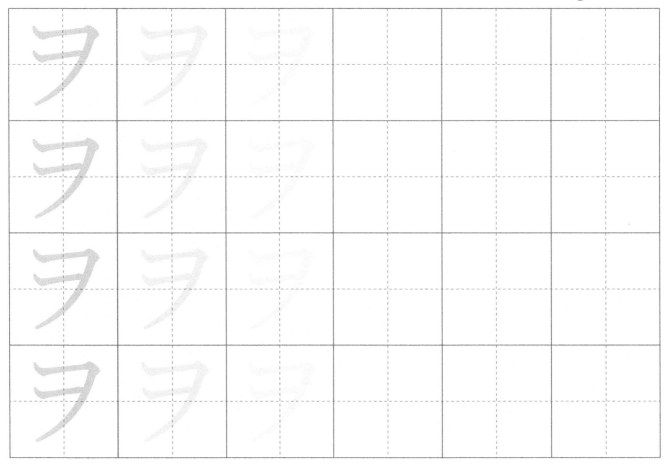

Now practice in these sets of smaller cells

ヲ ヲ
ヲ ヲ

ヲ ヲ
ヲ ヲ

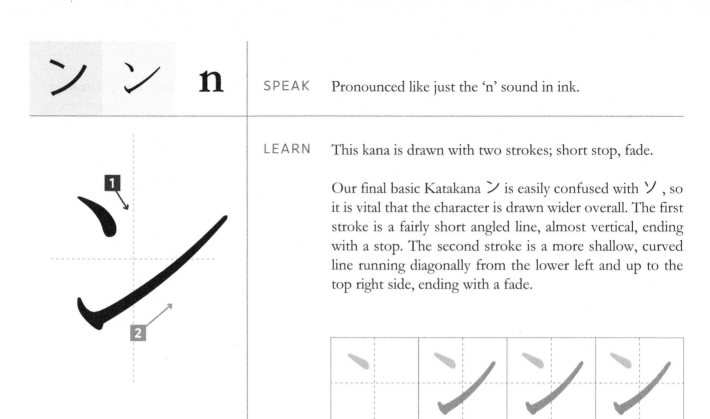

ン ン **n**

Pronounced like just the 'n' sound in ink.

LEARN This kana is drawn with two strokes; short stop, fade.

Our final basic Katakana ン is easily confused with ソ , so it is vital that the character is drawn wider overall. The first stroke is a fairly short angled line, almost vertical, ending with a stop. The second stroke is a more shallow, curved line running diagonally from the lower left and up to the top right side, ending with a fade.

WRITE

First, draw this character in the large cells below

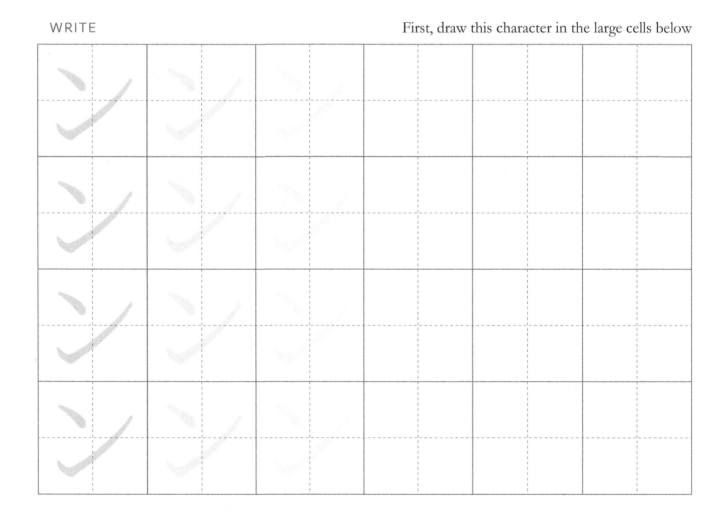

Now practice in these sets of smaller cells

Part 3

GENKOUYOUSHI

GRID PAPER FOR
FURTHER PRACTICE

Part 4

FLASH CARDS

PHOTOCOPY OR CUT OUT & KEEP

a

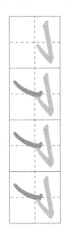

Pronounced like the 'a' in car or father, but shorter.

i

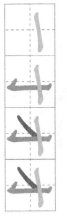

Pronounced like the 'ee' in eel.

u

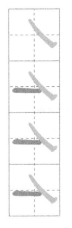

Pronounced like the 'oo' in zoo.

e

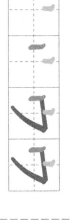

Pronounced as 'eh' like the 'e' in men.

o

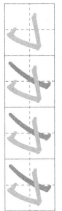

Pronounced like the 'o' in original.

ka

Pronounced like 'car' but without the 'r' sound.

ki

Pronounced like 'key'.

ku

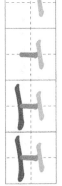

Pronounced like the 'koo' in cuckoo.

ke

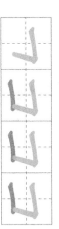

Pronounced like the 'ke' in Kenneth.

ko

Pronounced like the 'co' in core.

sa

Pronounced like the 'sa' in sardines.

shi

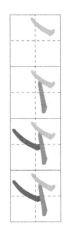

Pronounced like 'shee' as in sheet.

su

Pronounced like the 'su' in super.

chi

Pronounced just like the 'chi' in tai-chi.

na

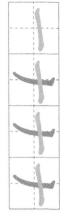

Pronounced like the 'na' in narwhal.

se

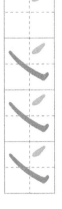

Pronounced like 'say' but with less 'y' sound.

tsu

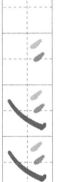

Pronounced just as the 'tsu' in tsunami, with a silent 't'.

ni

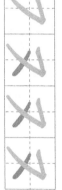

Pronounced like the 'nee' in needle but shorter.

so

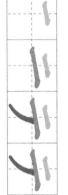

Pronounced like the 'so' in soy.

te

Pronounced just like the 'te' in ten.

nu

Pronounced like the 'noo' in noodles but short.

ta

Pronounced like the 'ta' in target.

to

Pronounced like the 'to' in tick-tock.

ne

Pronounced like the 'ne' in nest.

no
Pronounced like the 'no' in nose.

he
Pronounced like the 'he' in Helen.

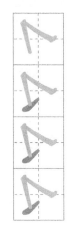

mu
Pronounced like 'moo' but in move.

ha
Pronounced as the 'ha' when laughing, like ha-ha.

ho
Pronounced like the 'ho' in home.

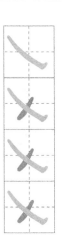

me
Pronounced like 'meh' like the 'me' in mend.

hi
Pronounced like the 'he' in He or She.

ma
Pronounced like the 'ma' in market.

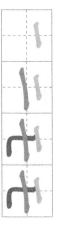

mo
Pronounced just like the 'mo' in more.

fu
Pronounced as 'hu' like the word 'who'.

mi
Pronounced just like 'me'.

ya
Pronounced like the 'ya' in yard'.

yu

Pronounced like the 'u' in universal.

yo
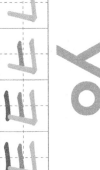
Pronounced just like the 'yo' in yo-yo.

ru

Pronounced like the 'rew' in brew.

ri

Pronounced like the 'ree' in reef.

re

Pronounced like the 're' in rent.

ra
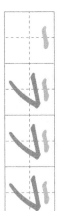
Pronounced like the 'ra' in ramen.

ro

Pronounced like the 'ro' in road.

wa

Pronounced like the 'wa' in wagon.

wo

Pronounced like the 'oh' in woah, with a silent 'w'.

n*

Pronounced like just the 'n' sound in ink.

ありがとう

arigatou

Thank you!

Thank you for choosing our book!

You are now well on your way to learning how to read, write and speak Japanese, and we hope that you enjoyed our Katakana workbook.

If you enjoyed learning Japanese with us, we would very much like to hear about your progress in a review!

We are always eager to learn if there is anything we can do to make our books better for future students. We are committed to making the best language learning content available! Please do get in touch with us via email if you had a problem with any of the content in this book:

hello@polyscholar.com

POLYSCHOLAR

www.polyscholar.com

Made in the USA
Monee, IL
28 December 2022

23940692R00077